THOM

THE

PRIVAT
TANK ENGINE

Midland Publishing
Limited

THOMAS
THE
PRIVATISED TANK ENGINE

Incledon Clark
Illustrated by Nick Clark

Midland Publishing and the Railway Development Society wish to make it clear that the content of this book does not reflect the views of the Rev W. Awdry or his publishers.

ISBN 1 85780 022 2

First published in book form in 1994 by
Midland Publishing Limited
24 The Hollow, Earl Shilton,
Leicester, LE9 7NA, England
Tel 0455 847 256; Fax 0455 841 805

Published in association with the
Railway Development Society, to whom
royalties from the book are being donated
to further their campaign for better railway
services in all parts of Britain.

Printed and bound in England by
Printhaüs Graphique Limited
Round Spinney, Northampton, NN3 4RD

Contents

6 *Foreword*
7 *Introduction: Railway Development Society*
8 Thomas and the advertised connection
10 Two platforms short of a station
12 Thomas goes racing
14 Thomas gets his sums wrong
16 Thomas runs non-stop
18 Thomas on the level playing field
20 The gravy train
22 The French Connection
24 Thomas's summer holiday
26 Thomas's day off
28 Thomas returns to his roots
30 A green and pleasant land
32 Hire prices
34 High spirits
36 Thomas goes nuclear
38 Just the ticket
40 Without a shadow of franchise
42 Thomas is grounded
44 Poll tax on wheels
46 Thomas on the warpath
48 April Fool
50 Thomas and the Passenger's Charter
52 The long arm of the lawyers
54 A Bridge Too Low
56 Thomas and the guarantee
58 Thomas takes a lunch break
60 Tunnel vision
62 All change
64 *What is the Railway Development Society?*

Foreword

Thomas the Privatised Tank Engine first appeared in the pages of *Private Eye* in January 1993 and rapidly established itself as a childish classic.

It was based on an absurdly simple idea. What if the Government were stupid enough to privatise the Railways? It could never happen of course but children love the unbelievable and incredible stories always become their favourites.

Such are the delightful tales of incompetence, shortsightedness and greed that make up this collection. They will transport you to another world – unlike the privatised trains which won't transport you anywhere. And whilst you're waiting for these trains not to arrive you'll find *Thomas the Privatised Tank Engine* the ideal book to while away those long hours (Surely 'days' ? Ed.) in the unheated customer service lounge.

So join Thomas and his friends on their journey downhill fast. Let the Grey Controller turn the clock back to the Victorian age and revel in the nostalgic feel of the nineteenth century railways of tomorrow. Next stop . . . er there are no stops.

So Bravo Thomas! Let's wave the flag, ring the bell and blow the whistle on the government!

Ian Hislop
Editor, *Private Eye*

Introduction

I hope you will find this book entertaining, and a fitting addition to the tradition of English satirical writing. The writer's aim, as in all such books, is not just to amuse, it is also to point out the dangerous effects of the Railways Act due to come into force on 1st April 1994.

From this date, twenty-six Train Operating Companies (TOCs) start operating, as 'shadow franchises', running trains over tracks owned by a new body, *Railtrack*. The government has also created a Franchising Director and a Rail Regulator, with their own staffs, and anyone can form a private company to run trains.

Estimates of how many private companies are queuing up to do this vary considerably. Government Ministers claim up to fifty have expressed an interest. The *Financial Times,* in August 1993, discovered seventeen, the majority of whom are actually bus and coach operators. Subsequent researches by the Railway Development Society, representing rail users throughout the country, revealed that many of the companies had only expressed a very general interest and had no firm plans.

British Rail, via its twenty-six shadow franchises, can still run trains. At first, the Government did not want BR to be able to bid against private firms to run services, even though Ministers had referred to BR as the most efficient railway in Europe! One Government spokesman even said on the radio that he feared BR would win most of the bids. Then a threatened revolt by Peers led by former Conservative Transport Minister Lord Peyton, forced Secretary of State John MacGregor to back down on this question and allow BR to bid – though the Franchising Director (appointed by Mr MacGregor) has the power to overrule such bids . . . (You may think, dear reader, that truth is stranger that satire . . .)

Public opinion was against the Government's privatisation plans. Up to 83% of those questioned were against it, according to one survey. Many MPs responded to expressions of concern from their electors and, as a result, further concessions were made by Mr MacGregor, notably on preserving the discounts available on most Railcards and ensuring that a national timetable is produced.

Well-informed public opinion can influence events, and that is a message of hope which this book suggests. But that opinion needs to be channelled constructively. Rail users need a voice. That voice is provided by the Railway Development Society and scores of local rail users' associations.

Since the passing of the Act, RDS has been in contact with would-be private operators, managers of the new shadow franchises and Railtrack officials, putting the users' point of view. We shall also be involved in close monitoring of services and facilities between now and the next General Election.

Trevor Garrod

Trevor Garrod
General Secretary, *Railway Development Society*

Thomas and the advertised connection

Gordon the Virgin engine was travelling very fast as he approached the big station one morning.

"Steady on!" yelled Thomas from his branch-line platform.

"We're going too fast! We're going too fast," shouted Gordon's carriages. And Gordon rushed through the station in a flash of gleaming white paint.

Thomas's passengers, who caught Gordon's train into the big city every morning, were very angry. They summoned the Fat Controller.

"Gordon does not stop here any more," he explained.

"But whyever not?" they cried.

"This stop is unremunerative. Cutting it out means Gordon can get to the big city three minutes quicker."

"Then how are we to get there every morning?"

"Turn right out of the station and a hundred yards on your left you'll find the Nissan car showroom. Thank you," he said, and disappeared into his office.

Thomas's train was empty next day, and at dusk the Grey Controller visited Thomas at his engine shed.

"I'm very considerably annoyed with you," he said, shaking his head. "Your train was empty this morning."

"That's because the Bearded Controller has forbidden Gordon to stop at the big station."

"Clearly there's no demand for your service," continued the Grey Controller, ignoring Thomas.

"That's ridiculous. My branch line serves a catchment area of 150,000 people," protested Thomas.

"I shall not let you burden the taxpayer like this. I shall put a stop to this very bad situation, oh yes."

Thomas brightened at these words. "Oh thank you, sir. I'm so glad you're going to make the Bearded Controller serve the population as well as his shareholders. I mean, what right has he to deprive ordinary folk of their train to work?"

"The Bearded Controller is a very rich man," said the Grey Controller. "And you, Thomas, are unemployed. Your branch line is closed as from tomorrow."

Gordon rushed through the station in a flash of gleaming white paint

Two platforms short of a station

"The Grey Controller says this station is too short," said Thomas's driver one afternoon as Thomas approached a country halt.

"Ah. It will be good to see the platform extended at last," replied Thomas.

As he drew up he saw the Fat Controller struggling to nail a notice to a lamp post. "Excuse me sir," said the Fat Controller to a thin man waiting for the train. "Would you be kind enough to fix up this notice? My doctor has forbidden me to knock."

The thin passenger's jaw dropped when the Fat Controller, panting and sweating, handed him the hammer and the notice. "No, I jolly well shall not!" he exclaimed. "What the devil do you mean by 'Notice of Closure'?"

"It is to be closed on safety grounds, sir. The train is longer than the platform."

"So what? I'll have you know I've used this station every day for fourteen years, and there's not a scratch on me."

"It is conceivable, sir, that one of our customers might injure himself by stepping out of a carriage door which is not opposite the platform."

"Nonsense!" said the thin man, climbing aboard Clarabel.

"I'm afraid the rules and regulations state that this station is too short, sir," said the Fat Controller. "And it's more than my job's worth to ..."

"I'll see you in court!"

The following Monday, Thomas sailed straight past the closed station. Then he saw a flashing blue light in a nearby road. "Look! An accident!" said Thomas.

Passing by, he saw the body of a thin man sprawled across the bonnet of a car.

"He won't be seeing the Fat Controller in court after all," said Thomas.

"Must have been walking to the bus stop," observed the driver.

"Will they close the road on safety grounds too?"

"Don't be silly, Thomas. Closing a road is more than anyone's job's worth, even the Grey Controller's."

"Look! An accident!" said Thomas

Thomas goes racing

"Oi, Grandad! I'll race you to the end of your branch line," shouted Bertie the Deregulated Bus over the station fence one afternoon.

Thomas thought 'Grandad' was a bit rich coming from Bertie. Rumour had it that Bertie was owned by Controllers of all shapes and sizes before the Greasy Controller bought him.

"I'm game," replied Thomas. "But when are you due to depart?"

"Due?!" laughed Bertie. "Due?! We don't bother with timetables no more. This is 1994 you know."

At 17.45 the guard blew his whistle. Thomas and Bertie were off.

Crossing over the High Street, Thomas saw Bertie fuming in a huge traffic jam. "You should get yourself some bus lanes!" he whistled.

But later Thomas came to a red signal.

"Sorry!" called the signalman from his museum-piece cabin. "Anyone got any sellotape? My Edwardian levers are falling apart."

And as he hunted for his screwdriver Bertie roared past on the new £40m Inner Relief Distributor Link road. "You wanna get yourself some rubber tyres!" he yelled.

Thomas had to be steadied once he was under way again. "You can't do thirty along here, Thomas," said his driver, applying the brakes. "Have you forgotten that landslip in 1954?"

But Bertie was nowhere to be seen when they reached the terminus at 18.10.

"I couldn't finish the race," said Bertie the next day.

"Ha, ha. Fell into a pothole, did you?" laughed Thomas.

"Naw. It was six o'clock."

"So?"

"We have to be back in the garage by six o'clock."

Thomas was speechless. "B ...But you can't stop running that early!"

"Oh yes we can, and we do," chuckled Bertie.

"But what about the passengers who want a night out, or are working late, or have travelled from afar?"

"Stuff 'em," said Bertie. "It's money that counts, and there's not much of it about after six. You'll soon realise that when the Greasy Controller gets his hands on your franchise! Ha, ha!"

He laughed heartily as he roared away.

Bertie roared past on the new £40m Inner Relief Distributor Link road

Thomas gets his sums wrong

A man in a pin-stripe suit approached Thomas as he waited at the terminus station one afternoon.

"Mind if I take a ride, Thomas?" he asked. "I've heard a lot about our, er, your branch line and I'd like to see things for myself before we, er, begin the development programme."

Thomas loved to show off his line to important people, and he chattered excitedly. "As you can see, the terminus is perfectly sited – bang in the centre of town."

"Ah yes, centre of town," said the pin-stripe man, taking a clipboard from his briefcase.

"In fact, some people come to the station to do their shopping – for socks, knickers and croissants."

"Shopping! Most exciting." The man wrote on his clipboard.

They set off, Thomas acting as guide and the man taking notes. "Here's the 1921 signal box – proper little museum piece, eh?"

"Mmm. Museum. Interesting."

Then the man started questioning. He wanted to know how much coal Thomas ate each day, and how much it cost. What was his driver's salary? How much did tickets cost?

"And how many passengers do you carry each day?" he asked, his brow severely furrowed.

"Oh, loads," replied Thomas. "Nine hundred at least."

"WHAT?!" yelped the man. "Stop! I order you to stop right here, and turn back immediately."

Thomas was frightened. He obeyed although he knew his passengers would be furious.

The pin-stripe man relaxed as they reversed back up the line.

"These are exciting times for your branch line, Thomas."

"Are they?" Thomas was bewildered.

"Yes. In three years' time it will be a smooth, fast dual-carriageway road. The terminus will become 'The Buffer Stops Centre', an in-town indoor shopping complex with ten-pin-bowling alley. And there's potential for a substantial residential development where your engine shed is."

Thomas felt sick.

"And that last station we passed will become a roadside taverna and nightclub complex."

How much worse could it get? thought Thomas.

"Annie will be parked there as a bar carriage, and Clarabel will become a linear discotheque hall. And don't worry, my boy, we shan't be sending you to the scrap heap either. No, you'll be the 'star' attraction, ha, ha, under your new name - 'Starlight Express'."

Thomas winced.

"You'll be the centre of the adventure playground. And you shall have a nice new coat of paint – red, green, pink and gold. And the whole complex will be called, let me see ... Chuffers."

Thomas had a nervous breakdown on the spot.

"You'll be the 'star' attraction, ha, ha!"

Thomas runs non-stop

"Hey! You've gone past my stop!" screamed a middle-aged shopper from Clarabel's front window.

"Sorry, madam," replied Thomas. "That one's a private station these days, and only express trains can afford to stop there. You'll just have to walk from the next public station."

But she had a better idea the following week. When Thomas was approaching her normal stop she pulled the communication cord. "Thank you," she said primly as Thomas screeched to a halt beside the platform in the private station.

"Look!" yelled Gordon the Virgin Engine from the opposite platform. "There's someone getting off a local train!"

Six liveried porters rushed to the shopper's assistance. They lifted her off her feet and stuffed her back inside Clarabel.

"She was wearing a plastic mackintosh!" spat Gordon. "How vulgar."

"All right, gentlemen, everything's under control," said the station public relations manager. He was attempting to calm all the double-breasted business travellers who had witnessed the spectacle, but they both looked in half a mind to make a dash for their BMWs.

Gordon was also visibly shaken. "And a carrier bag, too. Ugh!"

But the shopper got her own back. By the following week the platform where Thomas's local riff-raff used to alight had been hurriedly fenced off and turned into a city-centre car park. So now she parks her Lada on the station – and for half the train fare she used to pay.

"Look!" yelled Gordon the Virgin Engine. "There's someone getting off a local train!"

Thomas on the level playing field

"Now remember, Thomas," said the Fat Controller. "We can only keep this contract if we beat the lorries on price, speed, price, reliability, and price. I want you to do your very best."

Thomas remembered those words at midnight when he backed onto his trucks. Jacko the Juggernaut purred arrogantly alongside.

"You don't stand a chance," said Thomas. "Each of my 35 wagons holds nearly 100 tons, but you're only allowed less than 38 by law."

"Oh, I always take much more than 38 tons," replied Jacko.

"We're bound to win on speed, too. I mean you're restricted to 30mph on much of your route, aren't you?" asked Thomas.

"Pah! My driver's bloody skillful, you know."

Passing through the first village, Jacko had to mount the pavement, cracking paving stones and bending a road sign. "The council will pay for that," he laughed.

At the next hamlet a war veteran had a heart attack when Jacko passed by just a few yards from his bed. The man thought the Luftwaffe was bombing his bedroom.

As dawn broke, Jacko flattened a small boy delivering newspapers on his bicycle.

Later Thomas passed Jacko as he waited at a set of temporary traffic lights. "Bloody gas board," growled Jacko. "Why do they keep digging up the road to get at fractured mains?"

"Must add a small fortune to gas bills," agreed Thomas.

The next time they met up, Thomas was waiting in a passing loop.

"Just waiting for a fresh driver," explained Thomas. "Surely it's legally time your driver took a rest too? We've been going well over eight hours."

"We don't bother with that. My driver's got lots of experience – he's been in the game for eight months, you know." Jacko accelerated onto the motorway slip road.

Shortly later, Thomas heard a distant bang. Jacko had smashed into a motorway pile-up, the fireball from his highly-flammable load instantly incinerating all the people in the vicinity.

"Well done, Thomas," said the Fat Controller as Thomas took a well-earned lie-in next morning. "You did your best. But they beat us on price."

"Well, couldn't we accept less profit? I mean, eight percent is a bit much during a recession. Jacko would be happy with one percent."

"No, Thomas. The Grey Controller has said we must make eight per cent on our operating, maintenance and capital costs, or else give up the service to the lorries."

"One other thing," said Thomas as the Fat Controller turned to go. "What's that hissing noise I keep hearing?"

"Oxyacetylene torches."

"What's being cut up?"

"Those trucks you had yesterday. Can't afford to keep surplus equipment during a recession. Goodbye, Thomas."

"The council will pay for that," he laughed

The gravy train

"I want no flippant questions. These are important people, Thomas," said the Fat Controller. Thomas was waiting patiently with Ingrid the Inspection Saloon.

"Here's someone now." Three cars drew up beside the station. "That'll be the new franchise holder, with just a selection of his shareholders."

As they boarded, more limousines arrived. "And that's the Fat Director, with some of his staff," explained the Fat Controller.

"What do they do?"

"Keep tabs on the franchise holder. Ah, now here's the Fat Regulator, with assistants of course."

"So what's his job?" asked Thomas, bewildered.

"Keeping tabs on the Fat Director." By now Ingrid was groaning under the weight of so many important people.

"But who's paying for all these people?"

The Fat Controller paused. "Those who will benefit from greater private-sector involvement in the railways."

"Hooray! The Grey Controller is going to increase our subsidy after all."

"Thomas, I told you not to be flippant," frowned the Fat Controller. He darted an anxious glance at Ingrid, who was now sagging in the middle. "Now, who's this? Ah yes, it's the Fat Railman. He looks after the tracks and stations and signals."

"And I suppose someone will keep tabs on him?"

"Ah, now here's the Fat Health and Safety Executive."

"So if the Government won't pay, we'll have to put our fares up. And then nobody will travel with us, and we'll close down and these people will be out of a job. Is that so?"

"Sorry Thomas, can't stand around chatting all day," said the Fat Controller. But the moment he stepped aboard Ingrid there was a bang. One of her springs had snapped under the weight, and she was leaning at a drunken angle.

"Too many chiefs and not enough engines," muttered Thomas. The fitters had already been sacked, so all the important people got out and drove off to find their next railway.

"Too many chiefs and not enough engines," muttered Thomas

The French Connection

There was a strong smell of garlic as Thomas pulled into the main station one morning. At the opposite platform stood a very odd train.

"What the hell kind of train are you?" asked Thomas.

"I am Jean-Paul the Frog engine. Today I am miserable."

"Why?"

"Because today the Tunnel opened and from now on I will have to visit this backward, under-funded and dogma-driven country of yours every day."

"We're not backward, under-funded and dogma-driven," retorted Thomas. "We're the only country in Europe to have fully-privatised rail services."

"Precisely," said Jean-Paul with a laugh. "You English have a lot to learn. You still believe private capital can build railway lines."

Thomas blushed as he recalled the non-appearance of so many privately funded rail projects.

"You see, *mon ami*, I am designed to travel at 300 kilometres per hour," boasted Jean-Paul.

Thomas didn't know whether to believe him. It sounded very fast, but he had never heard of kilometres before.

"I've even got my own signalling system in my cab," said Jean-Paul.

"Rubbish!" said Thomas. "How could signals possibly fit inside an engine?"

Jean-Paul smiled patronisingly. "In my country, the state has built me fast railway lines, straight as an arrow. But here your old railway tracks are *merde* – all the bumps and curves are bad for my suspension."

"Don't you insult my railway," shouted Thomas. "I'll have you know it was built by George Stephenson himself, in 1834."

"Precisely."

"I'll show him, I'll show him," puffed Thomas as he left the station. "He can do what he likes in his country, but over here he'll jolly well play by our rules."

Next morning, Thomas smelt Jean-Paul behind him as he pulled into a little country station.

"Toot-toot, I'm an express service," called Jean-Paul.

"Not any more you ain't - you're in our country now," said Thomas, waiting for an old lady to find pennies for her ticket.

"Hurry along, hurry along," urged Annie and Clarabel.

"Plenty of time, plenty of time," yawned Thomas as he rolled from one wayside station to the next.

Sometimes Thomas would pretend to suffer sudden senile dementia – he was 40 after all. That would delay Jean-Paul for hours, because rationalisation meant there were no extra tracks to contend with emergencies.

And, sure enough, Thomas began to see a lot less of Jean-Paul after a few weeks. Jean-Paul was too slow.

"300 kilometres per hour, my wheel!" chuckled Thomas.

Instead, the passengers chose to go by plane or by car.

"Don't you insult my railway," shouted Thomas

Thomas's summer holiday

"This track's too bumpy," said Thomas, lurching cautiously along his branch line. "It's giving me a headache."

"Yes. Didn't you know our boys have taken a maintenance holiday?" said his driver.

"It's all right for some. When do they come back from the Costa del Sol?"

"Er, they won't be back, Thomas."

"What?"

"It's all part of bringing private enterprise into railway management – cutting everything but the fares."

The Fat Controller braved the rain that afternoon as Thomas took his nap. "Thomas, meet Selina the Sprinter Unit. She's taking over your branch line from today."

"Rubbish! She's not man enough for the job."

"You know we're an equal opportunities employer."

"But she's only two carriages long. How will all the summer holidaymakers manage?"

"The fact is, Thomas, she's a lot lighter than you."

"You! You ..." spluttered Thomas. "*You're* telling *me* I'm overweight?"

The Fat Controller turned red. "Look, Thomas. She'll cause less damage to the track during the maintenance holiday."

But once the Fat Controller had driven away, Thomas made his way to the station as usual, blocking Selina's access to the platform.

"I'm not having that fat bugger telling me to watch my boilerline," huffed Thomas indignantly as he made his usual journey up the branch line. "I'll show him who's too heavy ..."

But just then he started to feel unsteady. The rails parted beneath his wheels and he crunched to a halt.

Despite the rain, the passengers were happy to lend a hand with the jacks when they heard that the maintenance boys were on holiday. "They deserve a week off," said one lady, dishing out cakes and tea from a Thermos flask.

The Fat Controller raced up alongside."I told you to stay away from here!" he roared at Thomas from his car window. "Get back to the junction immediately!"

Selina the Sprinter Unit was waiting to take the passengers as Thomas returned sheepishly to the junction. "Hallo, Thomas," she said with a false smile. "Your P45 is in the Fat Controller's office."

The rails parted beneath his wheels and he crunched to a halt

Thomas's day off

"If I went on strike, this town would be brought to its knees," said Thomas as the passengers packed into Annie and Clarabel one morning peak.

"Shut yer face," said Bertie the Deregulated Bus as he moved off with just one passenger on board.

"I'm indispensable, you see," Thomas called after him smugly.

"Bad news," said Thomas's driver next morning. "Someone's committed suicide on the down fast line."

"Anyone we know?" asked Thomas. "The Fat Controller has been looking depressed lately. He keeps muttering things like 'open access' and 'vertical integration'."

But just then the Fat Controller waddled along the platform. "Yes, the line will be closed all day, while investigations are carried out."

"But that's not fair," said Thomas. "If someone was knocked down on a road, the police would keep the traffic moving past and clear the road in a jiffy."

"But Thomas, you know a death on a railway is a serious matter."

"Very well, I suppose I'll have to take the alternative route round the coast."

"No you won't Thomas. We haven't paid to use that track."

"But it's only used by three freight trains a week. Surely we can use it for a nominal fee," protested Thomas.

"No, we're putting Bertie on instead. We won't have to pay a bean towards the roads he uses."

"Bertie? Oh my God!" Thomas was mortified.

The Fat Controller turned to a passenger who was about to step aboard Clarabel. "Replacement bus today, sir. Just out on the forecourt there."

"What? That filthy old boneshaker? Can't you see I'm wearing a suit? Besides, I've got to be in town by nine," said the passenger, hurrying back towards the car park.

Then Bertie gave a rude honk as he moved away from the station, with four passengers on board. "Indispensable again today, are we?"

"But ... Bertie! Wait!" cried Thomas in desperation. "What have you done with the other 246 regular passengers of mine?"

But there was no reply. Bertie was roaring away. And soon, Thomas was left in a silence broken only by the squeak of the car park's exit barrier nodding up and down furiously.

"Replacement bus today, sir"

Thomas returns to his roots

"I can't go on like this," wheezed Thomas one evening. "I haven't had a check-up for months, let alone proper repairs."

"Very well, Thomas," said the Fat Controller kindly. "I'll give you a week off and you can get yourself some treatment."

"But where? The big factory was privatised years ago."

"Just shop around. Find the lowest bidder for the job."

The journey to the factory where Thomas was built was a long way for an old engine. And he was in for a shock at the end of it.

"What the hell ...?" whooshed Thomas when he saw the bulldozers and cranes smashing down the factory walls.

Eventually he found Shaun the Shunting Engine dozing in a rusty siding.

"Hallo, Thomas. What are you doing in this neck of the woods?"

"I've come for repairs."

"Repairs! Are you mad? The factory was closed down months ago."

Thomas thought he was having a nightmare. "But if the factory is closed, who's going to build the new trains?"

"What new trains? This country doesn't need any more new trains," said Shaun.

"You're pulling my wheel. I mean, the Imperial War Museum has been asking to buy me for ten years."

"How come? You weren't built till just after the war."

"That's besides the point. I look as though I've been caught in the blitz, don't I?"

Shaun had to agree.

"Therefore, my new private owners will soon be investing in my successor, Thomas Turbo," said Thomas.

"Thomas, you've got your chimney in the clouds. Do you think you're generating enough profit to justify investment?"

Thomas felt embarrassed as he realised he'd been taken in by the notion that privatisation meant private investment. He was still a little confused, however. "But the older we trains get the more it costs to maintain us, the more unreliable we become, and the more dispirited passengers we lose."

"Correct."

"So tell me, Shaun, why do you say the country doesn't need new trains?"

"Because there won't be any railways to run them on."

Shaun had always been good at explaining things.

Shaun had always been good at explaining things

A green and pleasant land

The sun was about to set on a golden summer evening as Thomas rolled into the junction station. A group of noisy Italian tourists waited on the platform.

"Check their tickets before they get on," Thomas told his guard suspiciously.

The guard frowned. "These tickets," he jabbed. "They are not valid on this train."

"You go to the big station, *si?*"

"Yes, but your tickets are for the main line. We are going via the scenic route."

"No, no. It say here, return ticket to big station."

"Yes, but you must use a red train. This is a blue train. You know, the colour blue, understand?"

"No, I don't understand. There is no red train till tomorrow."

"Yes, you must wait till tomorrow. Or else buy single tickets for the blue train."

"O mama mia!" Eventually they paid up, and Thomas was on his way again, climbing across the bleak moorland. At the next halt a couple of Dutch cyclists held out their thumbs.

"Is there any point stopping?" asked Thomas. As he squealed to a stop he began to explain. "Only one of you can use this train. We only carry one bicycle."

"What?"

"Bicycle. You know, a bike. Those things with two wheels."

"No, Thomas, you're wrong there," said the guard.

The cyclists looked relieved.

"We've already got one bike on board," continued the guard. "Sorry, no room."

"But the train is nearly empty! And we can't cycle all the way back to the city tonight."

"Sorry, rules is rules," the guard shrugged from his doorway as the train departed.

"Never cycle anywhere you can't cycle back from," called Thomas. "Obviously."

At the next stop some German hikers climbed out. "You mind the paintwork with those backpacks!" shouted Thomas.

"Vot paintverk? Now, vot time does the bus depart?"

"Why do you ask me? Do I look like a bus?" retorted Thomas.

"Nobody at the big station could tell us the time it connects. Ve must go to the hotel by bus - it's 14.3 kilometers away."

"I'd start walking if I were you," said Thomas, releasing his brakes.

"Vait! Do you have a phone ve can use?"

"No."

"You must know where the bus stop is!"

"Couldn't tell you."

Thomas rolled through the darkness in silence for a while. "Huh," he laughed scornfully. "Foreigners! They'll never understand transport in a million years."

"Never cycle anywhere you can't cycle back from," called Thomas.

Hire prices

"What do they think we are? Taxis?" spluttered Thomas. "Anyway, it's too dangerous to ply for hire these days. You never know who'll pick you up."

"Like it or not," said Gordon the Virgin Engine. "We're all being sold to three different private companies, so they can lease us back to the Fat Controller."

"What a pointless exercise!"

"No, Thomas. There's money to be made here. Now, when the Fat Controller comes to settle the lease you must insist on a very high fee, like all the rest of us."

"No way. The Fat Controller's already making a loss, you know."

"Listen, Thomas. The only way our new owners will make a massive profit is through us all insisting on high rental fees."

"But then we'd be operating a cartel!"

"Don't be silly. We're engines, not drugs dealers." Gordon cast a glance around the yard, then lowered his voice. "And before you start feeling sorry for the Fat Controller, let me tell you he doesn't think much of you."

"Rubbish! He told me I was his trusty steed."

"He's selling you for one pound."

"Come off it, Thomas. That's way above the market price," said the Fat Controller. "You can't charge those fees if you're 40 years old."

"You told me I was your trusty steed."

"That was 25 years ago, when I was trying to help you over your mid-life crisis. Now you've got varicose valve gear and bronchitis in your boiler."

But Thomas stuck to his guns.

"Very well. You'll regret this, Thomas. I'll get Gordon to pull the train instead, for half the price you're asking."

Thomas began to have misgivings once the Fat Controller left the engine shed. Perhaps this was another of Gordon's dirty tricks. He need not have worried, however, because the Fat Controller eventually returned with his tie aslant and beads of sweat over his face.

"It seems I don't have any choice," he quivered.

Thomas began to feel sorry for him, but then remembered the one pound.

"I'll have to pay that ridiculous fee for you." Then the Fat Controller marched off to his office, to draft a notice of immediate fare increases.

Thomas the privatised tank engine

"He's selling you for one pound"

High spirits

"It's not fair!" Thomas complained as he waited by a red signal at the junction. "The signalman keeps me here for five minutes every morning just so Gordon can get in front of me."

Just then, Gordon the Virgin Engine rolled past on the main line. "Poop, poop! Cheer up, little Thomas," said Gordon. "The Grey Controller has guaranteed your subsidy for three years."

"How come I have to wait for you to pass every morning?" replied Thomas.

"There's only one track, little Thomas. So we can't both run on it at the same time."

"But you pick up all my passengers at the station if you get there first."

"Thomas," sighed Gordon. "You really must learn how to enter into the spirit of open access."

Thomas's guard popped his head into the cab. "I've never known this to happen before."

"I have," said Thomas's driver. "It was common practice in Victorian times for rival companies to delay each other's passenger trains. They used broken down coal trains or biased signalmen."

Next morning Thomas's guard had a whip-round on Annie and Clarabel. The passengers gave generously when they heard of Thomas's plan.

As they reached the junction the guard gave a whistle and discreetly handed a parcel to the signalman. Thomas's signal changed to green immediately.

"Peep, peep! Cheer up Gordon," sang Thomas as he rolled onto the main line. "Your on-train jacuzzi is guaranteed for three years."

Gordon sulked as he waited at his red signal.

"Cheers!" the signalman called after Thomas. Taking a swig from his new bottle of whisky, he said, "Here's to the spirit of open access!"

"Cheers!" the signalman called after Thomas

Thomas goes nuclear

"You're a very naughty engine," said the Fat Controller. Thomas had formed a pact with Gordon the Virgin Engine, and they had agreed to accept through tickets from each other's lines so passengers would not have to book twice.

"Your agreement with Gordon was anti-competitive," he continued. "From now on, you shall only pull trucks."

"No I won't, sir."

"What did you say?"

"There aren't any trucks left. Everything goes by road now."

"Yes, well, I shall think of something."

That night, Thomas was sent to a huge concrete factory surrounded by hundreds of security guards. A man in dark glasses, who identified himself only as Controller X, whispered instructions to Thomas.

"Is that all?" asked Thomas. "Just one nuclear flask?"

"It's not 'just' anything. Thousands of lives depend on you delivering it safely."

Thomas was nervous when he set off, but he soon began to enjoy his journey. Every signal was green before he approached. He flashed past trains which had been shunted into sidings just so he could pass without delay. Gordon was furious when he saw that Thomas was the reason for the delay to his morning express.

Thomas glowed with excitement. "I'm tingling all over!" he cried. "I'd give anything to couple up to Selina the Sprinter Unit just now."

Suddenly the fun came to an end. Thomas was switched onto a rusty, weed-grown railway which twisted its way through the countryside.

"Hurry up!" yelled the armed security guard in Thomas's cab.

"I'll be the judge of my maximum speed, thank you," replied Thomas, picking his way along tracks which no longer receive any maintenance.

A special crane was waiting to lift the flask when Thomas arrived at the other secret factory.

"Where the hell have you been? You nearly sparked a nationwide security alert," said a man in dark glasses, known only as Controller Y.

"I had to check my speed on that branch line for safety reasons. Thousands of lives depend ..."

"Good heavens!" said Controller Y. "Safety reasons!" He paused for thought, then spoke into his walkie-talkie. "The railway's too unsafe for Thomas to take another flask back with him. Get me Jacko the Juggernaut. We'll send it by road instead."

Thomas was green, with envy presumably.

"Hurry up!" yelled the armed security guard in Thomas's cab

Just the ticket

"If you're going there I'd advise you not to start from here," said Thomas one winter afternoon. "You can only buy local tickets from this station."

"Rubbish! I bought long-distance tickets here only last year," said the unhappy passenger.

"Ah, that was in the bad old days of highly-subsidised nationalisation. But now we've been able to improve our ticket services, thanks to the climate of highly-subsidised private operation."

"Look here," said the passenger angrily. "I've waited half an hour at this station and I'm freezing cold because the waiting room is locked."

"Of course, you'll find a warm, inviting Business Club executive lounge at each of our main-line stations. That's another massive improvement only possible under ..."

"This station's a mess, it's unstaffed, and if you don't want to sell me a ticket I'll jolly well drive there in my car, thank you."

"Wait!" cried Thomas. "You can still buy long-distance tickets at 400 stations across the country."

"But can't you understand?" The passenger tapped his temple furiously. "I want to buy a ticket from *this* station. *This* is where I live."

"Just hop on board and the guard will sell you a ticket to the next station, where you can then book your long-distance ticket. It's easy."

The unhappy passenger had his credit card in his hand as he alighted at the next station. "Stop!" he cried, as Thomas began to depart. "You can't leave me here."

"You're the one who wanted to buy another ticket."

"But the next train is due in an hour!"

"Yes, that's right. Thanks to privatisation you can now book a ticket to anywhere in less than one hour. It's our new While-U-Wait booking service."

"This is a disgusting waste of my time," the passenger shouted after Thomas.

"Don't worry, that station has an unlocked waiting room," came the distant reply.

The station also had a taxi rank, as the unhappy passenger quickly discovered.

"Stop!" he cried, as Thomas began to depart. "You can't leave me here."

Without a shadow of franchise

"Take my advice," said Gordon the Virgin Engine. "Hide Thomas in his engine shed."

"That won't solve anything," said the Fat Controller.

"Not to worry. At least 49 more companies are interested," said the Grey Controller. "This one, for example."

An excited businessman climbed out of a limousine. "Yes, I'd love to take on a franchise," he said. "I'll need these trains as a stop gap, because I've decided to electrify the line."

"Ahem," coughed the Fat Railman. "It's up to me which lines are to be electrified, or not as the case may be."

"Oh. Well in that case ..." said the businessman, turning to go.

"No, wait!" The Grey Controller seized his arm. "Just look at the quality of these trains."

The businessman frowned at Thomas, then brightened as he saw Gordon. "Yes. I'll buy this one and refurbish him."

"Ahem," coughed Thomas. "You can't buy him or refurbish him, because we all belong to a leasing company. But they'll soon tell you how much you'll have to pay to hire us."

"This is nonsense! Now will you stop wasting my time?" Again he turned, but the Grey Controller held him back.

"A man of your considerable experience could bring improvements to this railway. You'd be so much better than the deeply inefficient Fat Controller here."

The businessman's frown melted. "Yes, I must admit I was planning some remarkable changes to the timetable."

"Ahem," coughed the Fat Regulator. "Only I can make remarkable changes to the timetables, thank you."

"Right, that's it. You can stuff your franchise!"

"Not so fast." The Grey Controller whipped out a pistol and held it to the businessman's temple. "You sign this document right now or I'll bust your brains. Oh yes."

"No way," said the businessman, tearing the paper to shreds. There was a bang and he fell to the floor.

"Bastard!" muttered the Grey Controller, making for his car.

"Two down, 48 more to go," said Thomas. "There's no cause for concern."

"I've had enough of your cheek," the Grey Controller quivered. "I shall impose costly new safety requirements on your line, oh yes."

Thomas turned white.

There was a bang and he fell to the floor.

Thomas is grounded

Thomas had seen plenty of scruffy things since coming to work in the big city, but nothing compared with the squat train who was sliding to a stop beside him.

"Good God, train! Don't you ever wash in the mornings?" asked Thomas. "And get yourself a coat of paint. You won't attract any passengers until you buck up."

But at that instant Terry the Tube Train's doors slid open and hundreds of passengers surged forward, fighting to get on board.

"Huh," said Thomas in disgust. "The people in this city have such low standards. I'd take a bus if I were them."

"You won't get far on a bus these days, guv," said Terry. "Deregulated last month, they was."

"Well, I suppose you're the ideal product for this riff-raff," admitted Thomas. "Cheap and cheerful."

" 'Ang a banger, mate. Cheap and cheerful? I'll 'ave you know it's 90p just to the next stop, and the last time someone laughed hon a tube train was in 1972. Soon got 'is 'ead kicked hin, of course." There were screams as Terry's doors rolled shut on passengers trying to board.

"So what old slum are you off to this morning, my friend?" asked Thomas.

"Slum?" yelled Terry as his motors began to whir. "You'd call the country's biggest hairport a slum, would yer?" Bursting at the seams, he slid into his tunnel. A woman's head was trapped by the neck in the doors.

"Put me onto the airport line," Thomas ordered his driver. "Let's get in some free-market competition. I'll beat him squarely on speed, comfort, price, capacity, convenience and customer care."

"No you won't Thomas. There's no surface rail link."

"How ridiculous! We were ready to build it years ago."

"But we have to wait for the private sector to borrow the money."

"Ah yes, of course. But why can't the public sector raise money for a rail project like this? It's bound to recover its costs pretty quickly, after all."

"Well, Thomas, the answer to that one is ... er ..."

And they thought about it all day. And the next day.

They still haven't come up with any sort of answer.

Hundreds of passengers surged forward, fighting to get on board

Poll tax on wheels

"I don't anticipate charging much for this line," said the Fat Railman as he climbed aboard Ingrid the Inspection Saloon.

"Yes, it's pretty quiet even in the rush hour," replied the Fat Controller.

"Actually, I'm more interested in the value of the infrastructure than in the passengers. A £50 track charge for each service would seem about right."

Meanwhile Thomas was backing up to Ingrid. "Who've we got here then? Someone else who wants to close our line?"

"Sounded like it just now," replied Ingrid.

So Thomas worked up a terrific speed - faster than the track allowed in theory. "Hurry along, hurry along," he called out as he reached 40mph.

At the next station the Fat Controller climbed out. "What the hell are you doing Thomas?" he hissed. "Its twenty from now on, do you hear?" Then he turned to the Fat Railman. "The rest of the track is so shabby we'll have to crawl along at twenty."

"Oh I don't know, sir," said Thomas. "The local authority upgraded some of the track last year."

"Now that's interesting," said the Fat Railman, returning to his seat. "Maybe £100 per service would be more appropriate."

Shortly Thomas drew up at another station. "No, Thomas, we're not scheduled to stop here," said the Fat Controller.

"I just wanted to show the gentleman how the county council has spent thousands of pounds on a new waiting shelter and platform surface. That's a vote of confidence in the future of our line."

"Fascinating," the Fat Railman muttered, reaching for his clipboard. "Let's say £120 then."

"Thomas, go and stand in that siding," said the Fat Controller, his face twitching with exasperation. "Now, sir, let me explain. The local population has already paid for these improvements through the poll tax. If I have to increase the fares, they'll be paying twice for the same improvements."

"Really? Well you've made your bed, now you must pay to lie on it," laughed the Fat Railman.

"One other thing," Thomas called from his siding. "The council is about to spend £3 million on new signalling for the line."

"How convenient!" smiled the Fat Railman. "I'll set the track charge at £150."

"Thomas, you're fired!" screamed the Fat Controller.

The Fat Railman looked up from his clipboard and said, "In that case, Thomas, how would you like a job in my firm?"

"Thomas, you're fired!" screamed the Fat Controller

Thomas on the warpath

"We don't need *that* any more," growled Thomas, before letting fly a 40lb shell. The noticeboard headed 'Validity of Saver and SuperSaver tickets' was smashed to splinters.

He moved on along the platform, crushing benches, lamposts and passengers under his caterpillar tracks. "Can I help you?" asked a man in a kiosk marked 'Connections'.

"Oh yes," cried the Grey Controller from Thomas's turret. "I'm looking for ways to transfer even more traffic from the roads to the railways. Ha, ha!" He sent a shell crashing into the kiosk.

Next the Grey Controller aimed the gun barrel at a signal. "Hang on, we need that for safety reasons," said Thomas.

"No, we don't have crashes on private railways," said the Grey Controller. "Fire!"

Suddenly Thomas stopped, and the Grey Controller stood to attention. A stream of enormous lorries roared past. "Heil 44-tonner!" yelled the Grey Controller, thrusting out his right arm.

Annie and Clarabel were dozing in a siding. "Ach, bloody rural trains," screamed the Grey Controller, before smashing them to bits.

"What on earth is all this noise?" demanded the Fat Controller.

"Ve have vays of forcing you into retirement, oh ja!" The Grey Controller turned the gun barrel to face the Fat Controller. "You have for the railvays vorked for more than six months. So you have given us no choice but ..." And the Fat Controller exploded as a shell hit his stomach.

"And now," the Grey Controller shouted as Thomas lurched forward, "Ve vill destroy all der train factories, all der stations on prime city-centre land, all der rail unions, all der ..."

Beads of sweat ran down Thomas's boiler casing as he woke with a shiver. "Thank Brunel for that," he said with relief. "It was all a dream."

"Ve have vays of forcing you into retirement, oh ja!"

April Fool

"We electrics are definitely superior," said Edwina the Electric Train one rush hour.

"Rubbish!" snorted Thomas.

"We can reach parts other trains can't."

"Such as?"

"Such as the new tunnel they're going to dig right across the big city."

Thomas laughed. "Did you hear about those Boeing 747s being replaced by pigs on charter flights?"

"No, no," said Edwina earnestly. "They're going to make a full-size tunnel from the east to the west. It'll have five stops right beneath the city centre."

"You should become a science-fiction writer."

"And it will allow trains to run from the eastern outer-urban network through to the western."

"How much might this 'tunnel' of yours be costing, then?"

"Oh, about £1.8 billion."

"Ha, ha. And who's paying for it, the Fat Controller?" laughed Thomas.

"No, no. The government, the taxpayers."

"Come off it, Edwina. Where do you think this is, Europe?"

"Well, yes. We're in the EC aren't we?"

"So we made a bet," said Thomas.

"What on?" asked Claire the Cleaner, leaning on her broom handle.

"If the government committed £1.5 billion to this tunnel by April the First then I would buy Edwina a megawatt of electricity generated by renewable sources. If there was no sign of any such commitment by then, she would get me a crate of mineral water."

"Very clever."

"Cheers," said Thomas as Claire poured mineral water into his water tanks.

"Yes," said Claire. "Here's to the government's stinginess and indecision."

"Here's to the government's stinginess and indecision."

Thomas and the Passenger's Charter

There has been trouble on Thomas's railway lately. Monday was Thomas's fortieth birthday. He woke up stiff after the weekend. "I've got arthritis in my valve-gear," he groaned. And all day he lost time because he was aching so.

On Tuesday the morning train was cancelled because the guard was off sick. "We can't afford to employ spare guards," said the Fat Controller.

On Wednesday Thomas was delayed because the Victorian signalling system was up the creek again.

On Thursday the fares were increased, reflecting 'recognisable improvements to services' on Thomas's line.

On Friday Clarabel's brakes seized up, due to old age. "We can't afford to keep spare carriages," said the Fat Controller. The passengers were furious when they all had to pack into Annie like sardines. Waiting for the delayed guard, a group of angry passengers gathered round Thomas, demanding compensation and waving a pamphlet in his face.

On Saturday the Fat Controller brought the Grey Controller to Thomas's engine shed.

"I am very considerably annoyed with you, Thomas," said the Grey Controller, shaking his head and jabbing a finger at Thomas. "Your performance standards are very poor, oh yes."

"But it's not my fault," stammered Thomas. "Do you think I could have a twentieth-century signalling system? It is nearly the twenty-first century after all."

"Don't be cheeky, Thomas," said the Fat Controller sternly.

"Look at all these complaints." The Grey Controller waved a bundle of letters in Thomas's face. "You're going to cost the taxpayer thousands of pounds in Charter compensation."

"Well couldn't that money buy the new Thomas Turbo train, which has been on the drawing board for two years?"

"Thomas!" shouted the Fat Controller.

"We're going to stem these losses, oh yes," said the Grey Controller. "We've carefully studied all the options."

The words sent a shiver down Thomas's boiler tubes. "You mean you're going to privatise me?"

"Oh no. We're going to close your branch line," said the Grey Controller, and walked away.

And Thomas began to cry.

"Look at all these complaints."

The long arm of the lawyers

"That's criminal!" shrilled the woman with the suitcase. "It's three times more than the SuperSaver I used to buy."

"The law only requires us to provide through tickets at the full price," replied Thomas. "So we've abandoned the cut-price tickets like SuperSavers."

"But fares are supposed to drop with privatisation."

"They have. Our first class return, for example, is now three per cent cheaper - a change welcomed by such first class passengers as politicians, and financial consultants who specialise in privatisation projects."

"I'm not paying that sort of money." The woman stormed out of the station. "It's daylight robbery."

Thomas was startled when he next returned to the station. On the platform was a lawyer.

"Don't worry, Thomas, I'm on your side. I'll be defending you."

"A ... Against what charges?" Thomas quivered.

"Track maintenance charges, leasing charges, access charges, investment charges ..."

More lawyers trooped from the car park to the platform, which had by now been sealed off to the public. "You may recognise some of these chaps, Thomas. Many of them wrote reports on the best way to privatise your industry."

"So who's paying the charges for all you lot?" asked Thomas.

"Oh, my fees are very reasonable. £200 an hour, plus expenses. I'll need some extra pairs of hands, but they won't cost much. Now, the chap on the left is representing the Fat Railman, who will of course be paying his fees, the one next to him represents the Fat Regulator ..."

"But where does the Fat Railman get his money from?" asked Thomas in disgust.

"That's something we hope to thrash out over the next four months of negotiations." The lawyer climbed onto a platform trolley and clapped his hands for silence. "Afternoon, gentlemen. We've got a lot to do, so I suggest we knuckle down straight away. The Busy Lizzie Bistro is just to your left outside the station. I booked a table for 98."

They began to file out. Thomas's lawyer yelled, "By the way, chaps, I recommend the '86 Cabernet Sauvignon."

Thomas was left to ponder how on earth he would make both ends of his branch line meet in future.

"Afternoon, gentlemen. We've got a lot to do."

A Bridge Too Low

"Ho, ho! Look who's got too big for his tyres!" said Thomas during an emergency stop. The track ahead was buckled and down below was Jacko the Juggernaut - wedged under a railway bridge. "You've already poached all our freight, Jacko, and now you're trying to carry off our railway track as well, eh?"

Thomas's laughter was cut short when the Fat Controller arrived. "Rail services suspended for a fortnight," he panted.

"But last time this happened we had two trains - one each side of the bridge," Thomas complained.

"We can't afford to hire rolling stock from someone else." And he called out to the passengers, "Hurry along, please. Your bus is just off to the left, thank you."

Thomas returned to the big station, where the Grey Controller was getting into his car. "Hey," called Thomas. "There's trains lying around but we're hiring a bus because the trains belong to a different part of the company."

"Your rail network is deeply inefficient," said the Grey Controller.

"Can't you see this accountancy-led system is turning people back to their cars? They pay to go on a train, not a bus."

"That system means we can identify the true costs involved in running a railway, and make sure those costs are attributed to the right people."

Three months later Thomas noticed Jacko parked outside the magistrates' court.

"You're a very naughty lorry," said the magistrate, standing before him. "Your stupidity in driving at a bridge which you should have known was too low for you caused great disruption to road traffic. My husband had to drive the long way round - it took him an extra twenty minutes and he was late for his tea." She peered at Jacko over her glasses. "Therefore I am fining you £150, so you won't be so careless in future."

"What about the costs?" Thomas called out.

"Silence! I am also ordering you to pay £30 costs. Now is everything clear?"

"Absolutely, ma'am" said Jacko with a grin.

"What about the true costs?" shouted Thomas. But his words were drowned by the noise of Jacko revving up and the magistrate coughing.

"Ho, ho! Look who's got too big for his tyres!"

Thomas and the guarantee

Bertie the Deregulated Bus was almost in tears when Thomas arrived at his branch line terminus one evening. "I'm going to the scrap heap," wailed Bertie. "The county council has withdrawn my subsidy."

"Well, what else would you expect from a tax-capped Red Party council?" said Thomas. "The Blue Party, on the other hand, has said my subsidy is guaranteed, because I'm a socially necessary service."

"I was socially necessary," Bertie moaned as he left on his last service. "But now I'm going to the scrap heap."

Then Thomas noticed the Grey Controller and the Fat Controller talking in the shadows by the permanently closed booking office, darting shifty glances at Thomas. Soon the Grey Controller sped away in his car, and the Fat Controller approached Thomas.

"For operational reasons, we're going to make some adjustments to the timetable," he said. "Your morning run into town will be 40 minutes later, arriving at 9.20."

"But that's long after my passengers start work," protested Thomas.

"Quiet, Thomas! Your evening run will leave town at 4.50 instead of 5.30. Understood?"

"But ..."

"Good night, Thomas."

All the stations were deserted as Thomas puffed through the Monday morning drizzle. Only two old ladies going shopping climbed aboard, wet and furious because they weren't told of the timetable change.

Annie and Clarabel were empty on the evening return run. The two old ladies had forgotten to ask for a copy of timetable amendment supplement no.1035/AS4-Q and had missed the train.

The Grey Controller was waiting on the platform when Thomas arrived at the terminus. "Your subsidy shall be withdrawn," he said sternly.

"But you said subsidy would be guaranteed for socially necessary services."

"That is absolutely the case. But you are considerably not socially necessary. You were empty just now."

"But my timetable was changed ..."

"It is entirely a matter for the Fat Controller how he chooses to run his railway or not."

"So what do I do now?"

"You are going to the scrap heap. Oh yes."

Only two old ladies, wet and furious

Thomas takes a lunch break

"It's important that you understand this," said the Fat Controller while Thomas waited for a green signal. "I'm always watching my bottom line."

"Couldn't button your trousers this morning, eh?" muttered Thomas.

"What?"

"I said – we've always followed sound business principles."

"Yes, Thomas. Now, to make sure the books continue to balance ..."

"Sorry to interrupt sir, but aren't we forgetting something? If we devote too much attention to our profit margins we may forget we are really here to provide a train service."

"Yes, that's the idea. Er, no. No, what I mean is we have to stay on our toes ..."

"Sorry, you're missing my point sir. It's time for my midday service, but my signal is still red."

"Yes, I was coming to that." He paused. "Thomas, we're not running the midday service any more, for sound business reasons."

Thomas instantly decided on mutiny – he would pass the signal at danger. But then he saw a big black car accelerating away from the yard. Behind the tinted windows sat the Fat Railman.

"Ah, I get it," said Thomas. "The midday run was economic last month because we owned our own track and stations."

"Well, you must remember ..."

"But this month the Fat Railman owns our track and stations, and he's also taking a keen interest in his bottom line. He's charging so much for us to do the midday run that it's suddenly losing us money."

There was an awkward silence. The Fat Controller was shocked at Thomas's grasp of sound business principles.

"So what happens now?" asked Thomas.

"Just wait till the evening rush hour. It's only five hours away."

"And Annie and Clarabel?"

"Yes."

"And my driver? And my guard, and the signalmen and station staff?"

"Yes. Look, Thomas, don't worry about your midday passengers. They'll be all right – one doesn't have to pay access charges on the roads, you know."

So Thomas gave in and spent the afternoon contemplating Selina the Sprinter Unit's bottom line.

Thomas spent the afternoon contemplating Selina's bottom line

Tunnel vision

"There's something horrid in the tunnel!" wailed Selina the Sprinter Unit one afternoon.

"Oh, that'll be Jacko the Juggernaut trying out a new short cut," replied Thomas. "I'll soon flush him out." He uncoupled from Annie and Clarabel and puffed into the tunnel.

Seconds later he backed out at speed. "Robert Stephenson! There's a dogma blocking the tunnel!" he cried.

Even the Fat Controller was mortified. Selina became hysterical. "If the dogma doesn't go away our branch line will be isolated from the rest of the rail network. We'll starve. We're all going to die!"

The Fat Controller took charge. "Thomas, run along to that scrapyard and see if they've got any of those things left. What did we used to call them?"

"Trucks, sir?"

"Yes, that's it." And soon Thomas plunged into the tunnel again. This time he was pushing a truck, in which the Fat Controller stood bravely.

"Now listen here," the Fat Controller called into the gloom. "Most other countries are perfectly happy with nationalised railways."

"We will bring to the railways the considerable benefits of private enterprise," came the reply.

Thomas's driver said, "It must have escaped from Adam Smith's think-tank circus."

The Fat Controller tried again. "Your franchising system is going to fritter away millions of pounds on extra bureaucracy."

"We will make the rail network considerably more efficient," echoed the response.

"It's no good. I'll have to use the only language it understands," said the Fat Controller.

"Why don't we throw some cold water over it?" suggested the driver.

"Look here!" shouted the Fat Controller. "You're two apples short of a picnic! Public opinion does not support your franchising plan! Understand?"

There was a long silence, then the grey fog began to clear. "Bastards!" the tunnel echoed faintly, and Thomas thought he heard, "We're still going to cut your subsidy in half." Then at last there was light at the end of the tunnel.

Back at the station the Fat Controller announced, "We apologise for any inconvenience caused by the delay. This was due to a logic failure in the tunnel."

"Now listen here," the Fat Controller called into the gloom

All change

"Sorry, Gordon. I haven't got time to hang around in stations," said Thomas one afternoon. "This Shuttlelink initiative is a job and a half."

"Pah!" snorted Gordon, who was waiting to pull the teatime express. "It's only a 20-minute journey to the airport. Besides, that Shuttlelink nonsense is just a hollow ploy to dissociate the airport service from the rest of the rail network."

"Whatever it is, it's working," replied Thomas as he puffed away happily.

He was right. That evening the Fat Controller said, "Well done Thomas. You've helped make my Shuttlelink a success. In fact it's so successful we can afford to make a massive improvement to the quality of service we deliver."

Thomas couldn't sleep all night because he was so excited at the prospect of capital expenditure. He wondered what massive investment the Fat Controller had in mind - why, he might even provide new signs for the station platforms, or give the staff new name badges.

He discovered the answer when he rolled into the station the next morning, to find Gordon in the Shuttlelink platform.

"That's right, Thomas," beamed the Fat Controller. "We can afford to hire Gordon and his carriages, to give the customer-base the ride comfort it expects from our product."

"But it's only a 20-minute journey," protested Thomas. "Gordon is designed for the four-hour express run."

A look of panic spread over the Fat Controller's face.

"Besides, who is going to take care of ..."

"Yes, yes, Thomas. Stop blathering and give me time to think," snapped the Fat Controller.

"Oh, please let me rest," moaned Thomas. "You know I wasn't designed for this sort of thing."

"Sorry, but this is the non-stop express," replied Thomas's driver sympathetically. "And we're already an hour late because you're only doing seventy."

"We're going too fast, we're going too fast," clattered Annie and Clarabel. "We haven't a buffet car, we haven't a public address system, we haven't air conditioning ..."

Gordon was just about to leave with the Shuttlelink when Thomas arrived at the big station. "Chop, chop, little Thomas. Can't wait around in stations, can we?"

Thomas didn't reply. He had collapsed from exhaustion at the buffer stops.

He was barely conscious when the fitters dragged him to the engine shed and proceeded to stuff him with anabolic steroids and generally prepare him for the teatime express.

He had collapsed from exhaustion at the buffer stops

What is the Railway Development Society ?

The RDS is the only national pro-rail pressure group independent of both British Rail management and trade unions. It was formed in 1978 by the amalgamation of two long established voluntary associations, and today acts both as a campaign for a fairer share of transport investment for the railways, and as a consumer organisation representing rail users nationwide. It is not linked with any political party, and has members of all shades of political opinion.

We seek a better rail system for Britain because we believe that railways offer a safer and more fuel-efficient alternative to the uncontrolled growth of road transport for both passengers and freight; they are also much less damaging to the environment of towns and countryside, and to the health and safety of our citizens. We also believe that rail users need a voice to speak up for their interests, both with BR management and with local and national politicians who take far reaching decisions affecting their daily lives.

As campaigners we have pressed, with some success, for further electrification of the rail network; for better local and regional trains; and for the reopening of lines and stations closed to passengers. We have strongly opposed rail cuts and closures and have been at the forefront of opposition to the damaging aspects of rail privatisation. We have also done a lot of work in helping to promote the transfer of freight traffic from road to rail. The Channel Tunnel, a vital link with the rest of Europe, is a project which we strongly support.

As a consumer organisation, we have made many specific representations to BR, at local and national levels, in order to prevent deteriorations in services and to secure improvements wherever possible. We also act as a national advisory and co-ordinating body for the many local rail user groups, holding a conference of such groups every year. We also maintain links with other bodies campaigning for better public transport, such as Transport 2000, the National Council on Inland Transport, and Friends of the Earth.

Our quarterly journal, *Railwatch,* is read by many interested parties outside as well as inside the RDS, as are our local branch newsletters. We publish books, reports and leaflets on particular issues, as well as a series of regional guidebooks for rail passengers, which have become widely popular with the travelling public. If you would like to know more about the RDS and rail users' associations, please write to the RDS Membership Secretary at 13 Arnhill Road, Gretton, Corby, Northants, NN17 3DN. The 1994 standard membership rate is £10; juniors, senior citizens, unemployed £5; family/corporate rates on request.

As a voluntary body financed almost entirely from members' individual subscriptions, we cannot match the power of the roads lobby. Nevertheless, we have made sure that the case for railways is heard, and we are determined to continue pressing for a better future for rail transport in this country.